Welcome

To The Sport Cars Coloring Book

This Book

Belongs To

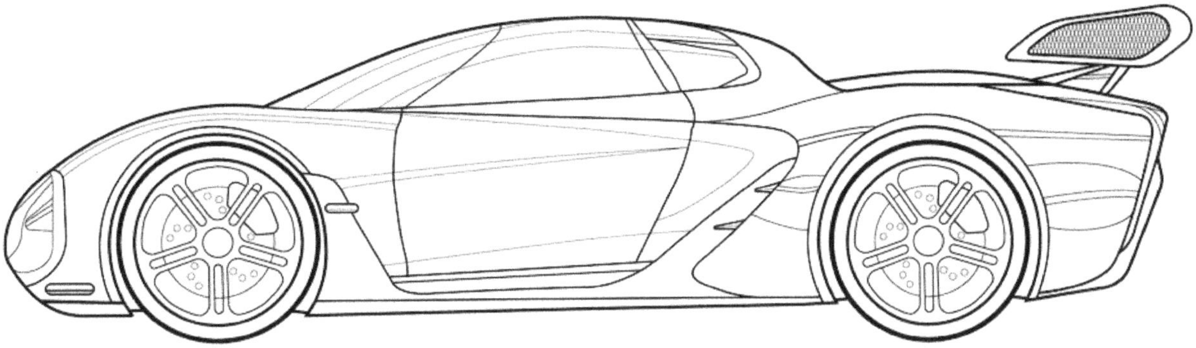

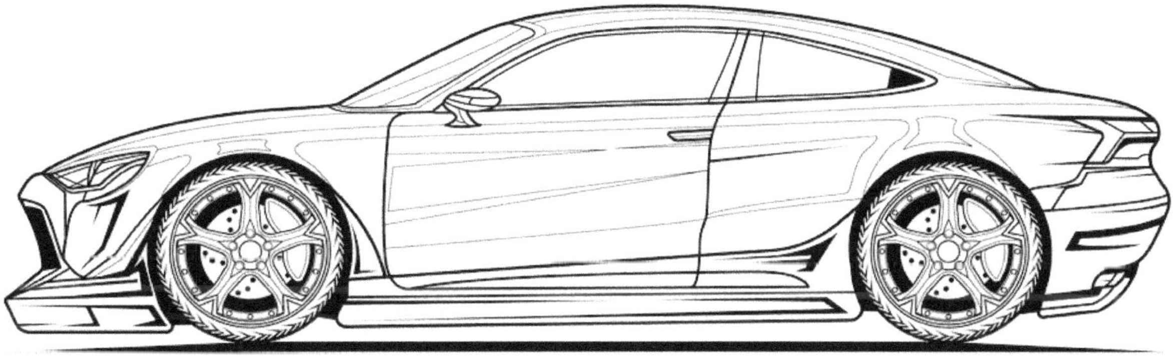

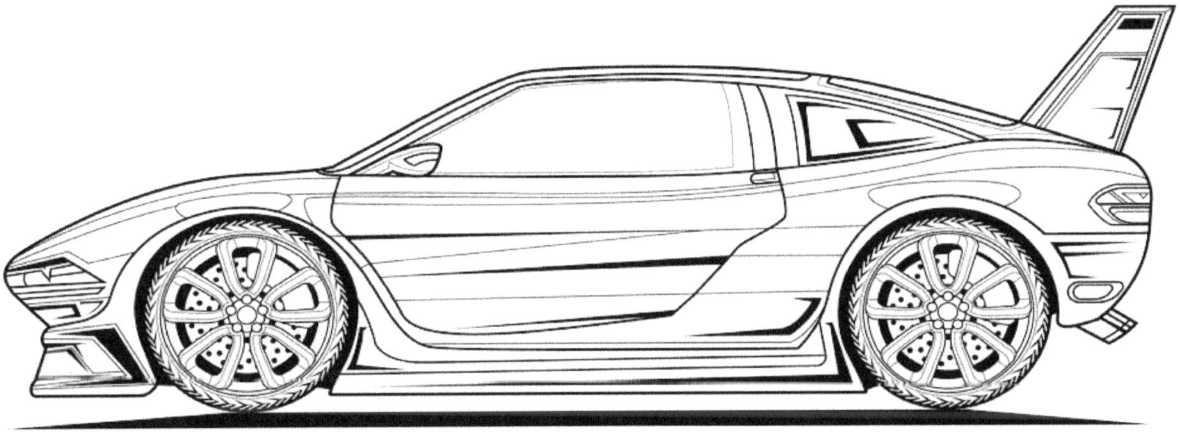

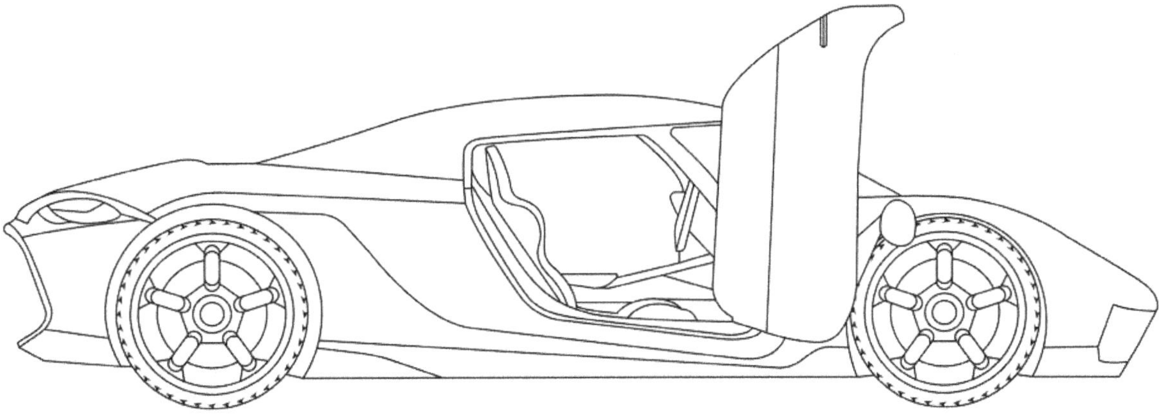

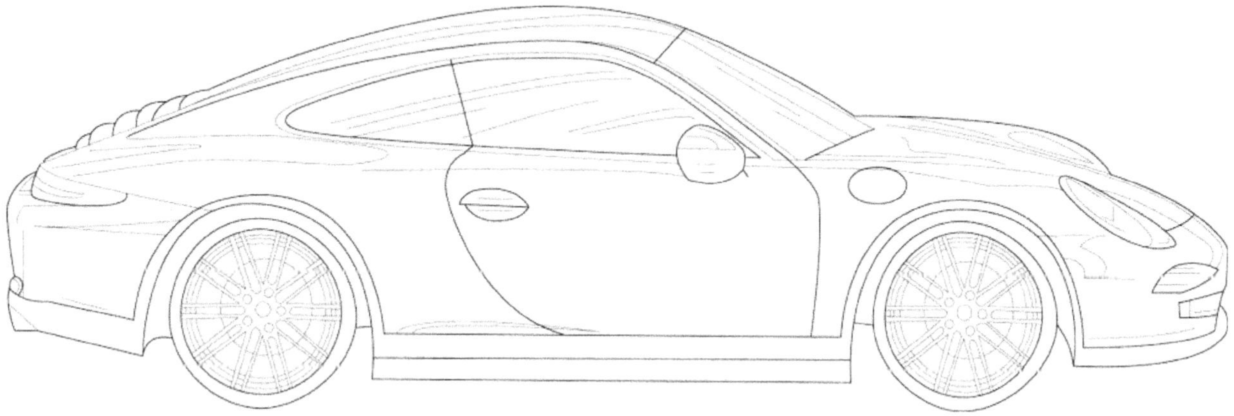

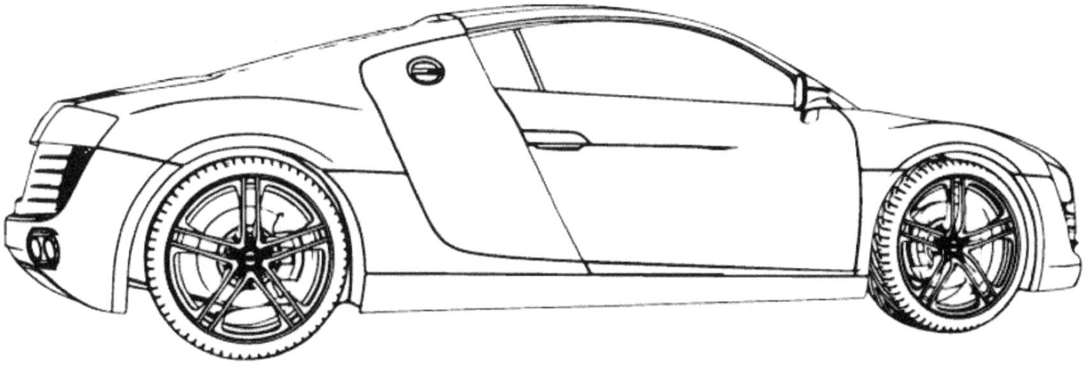

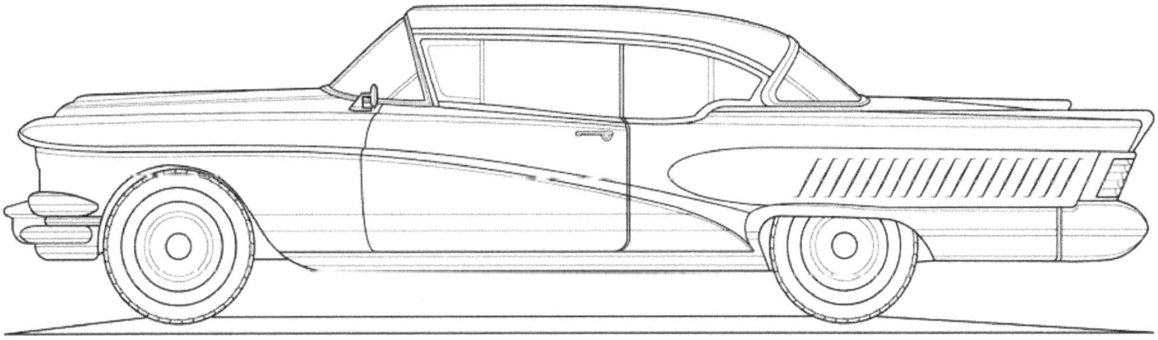

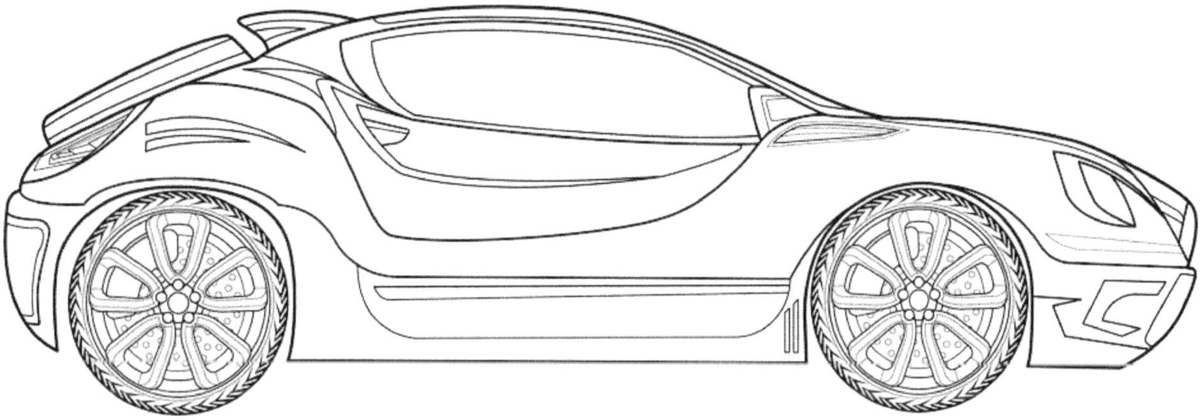

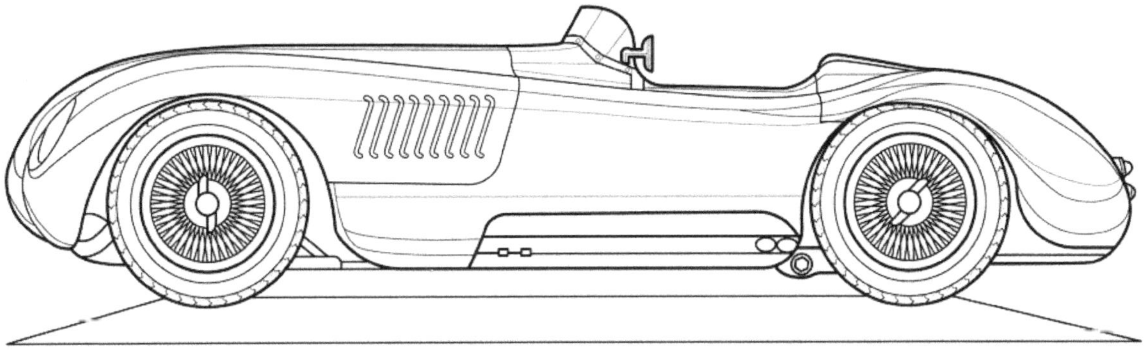

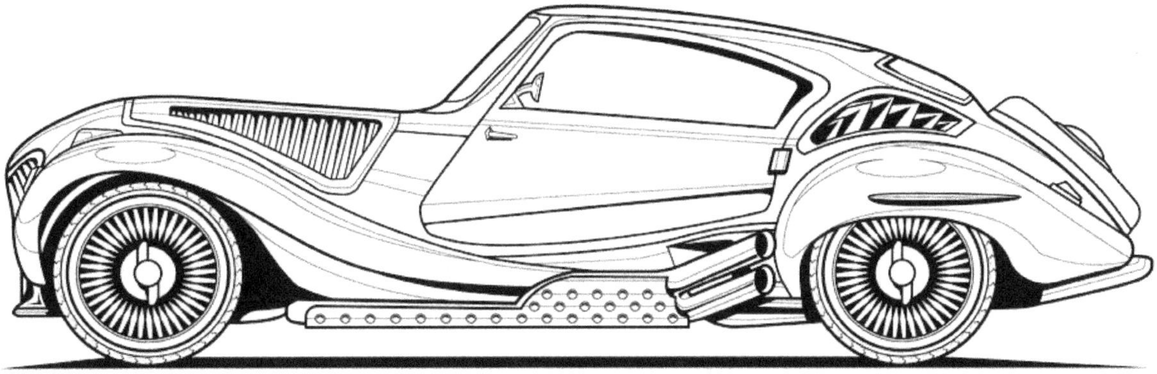

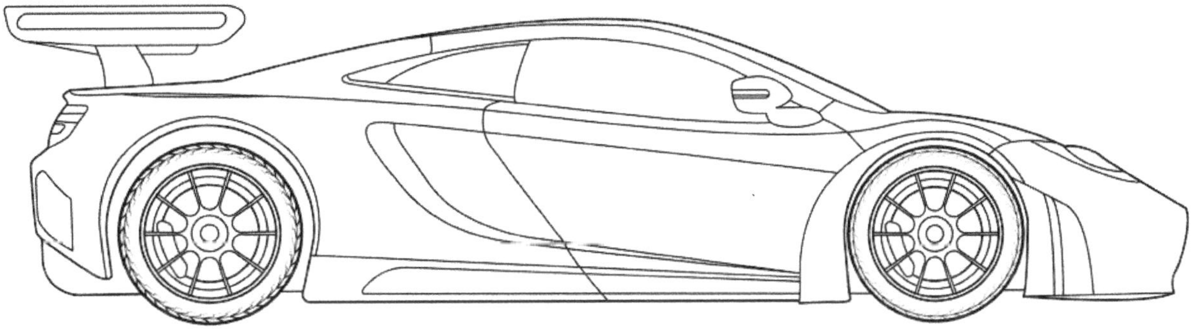

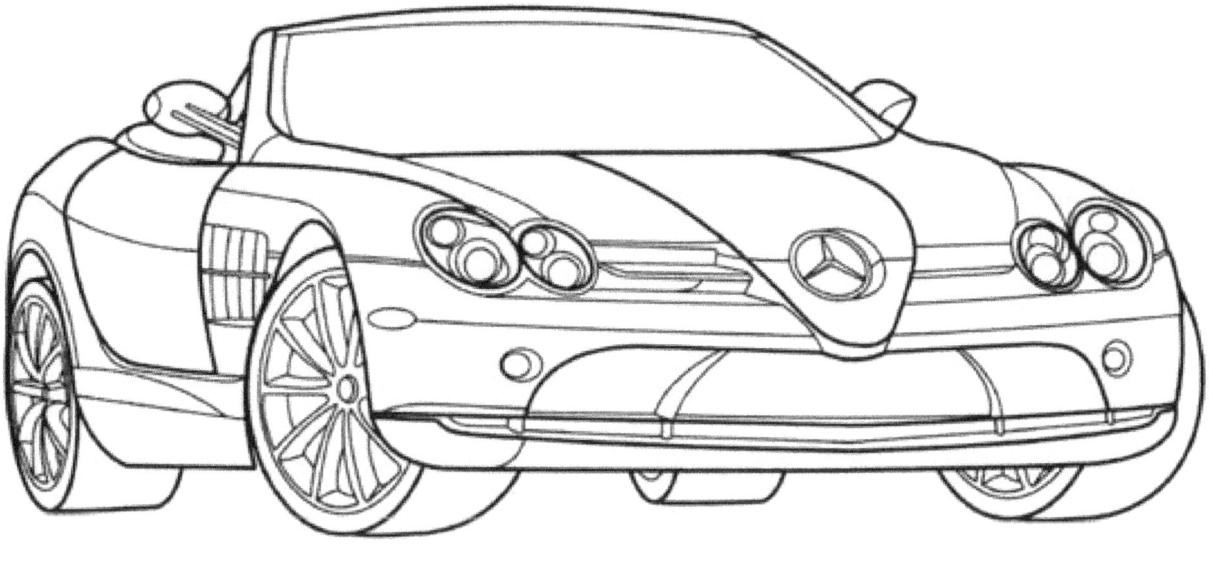

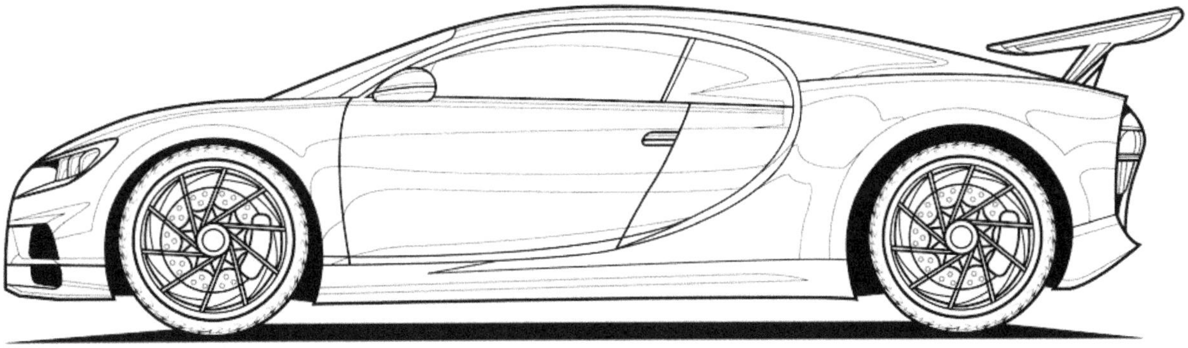

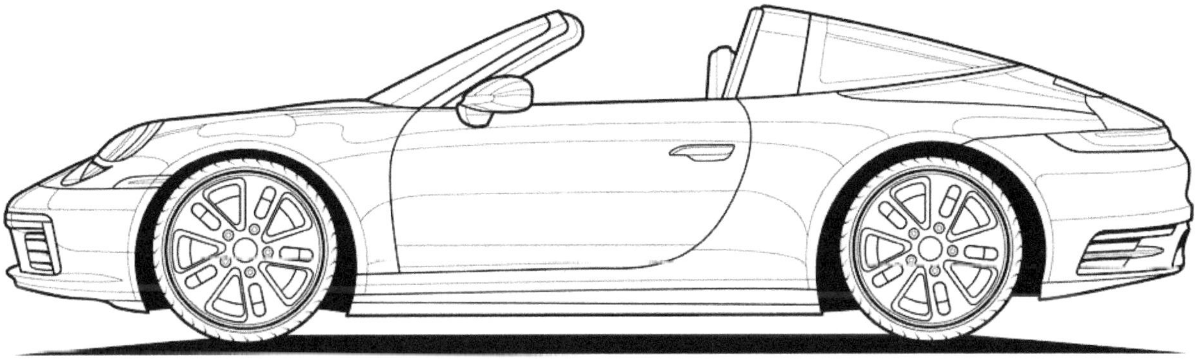

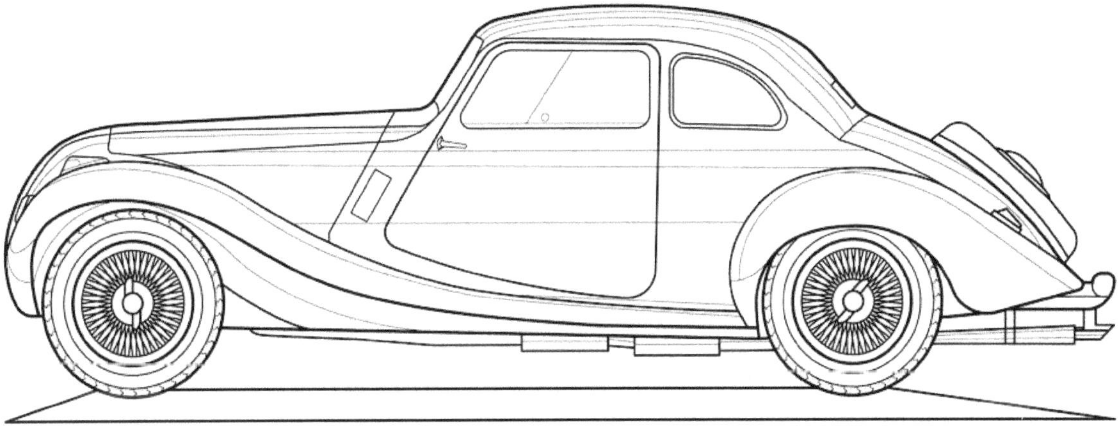

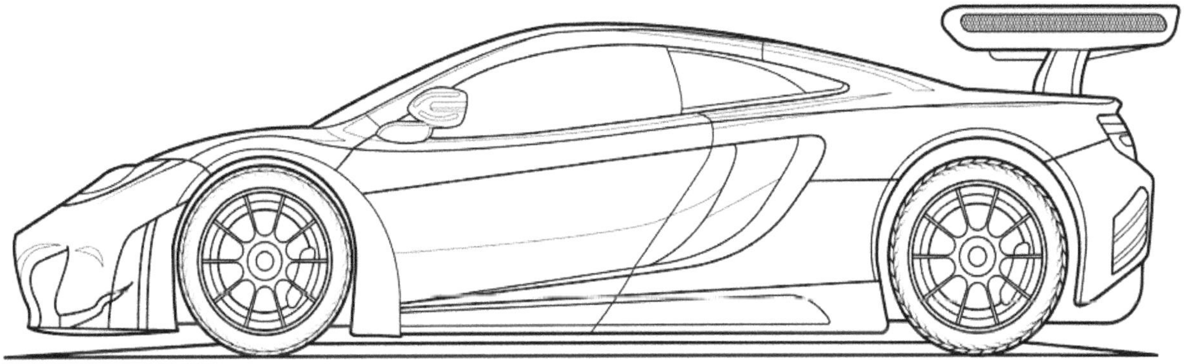

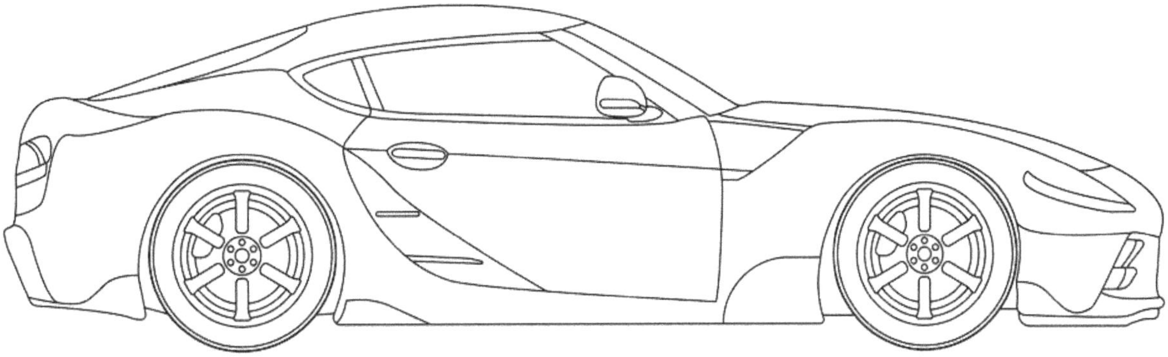

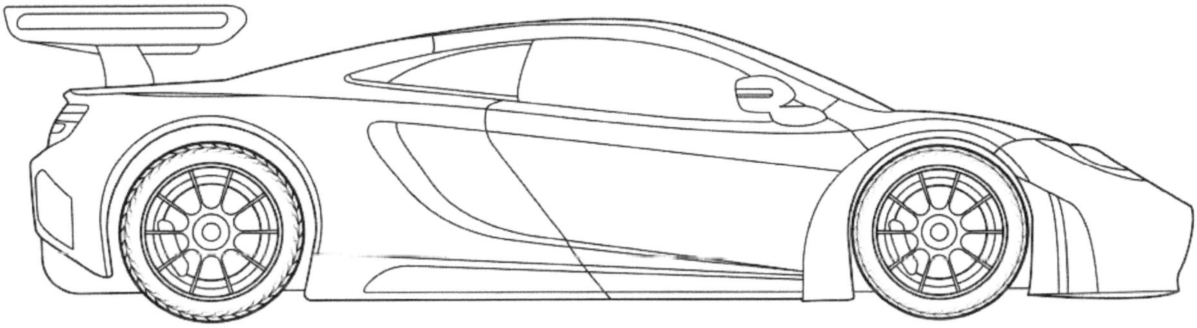

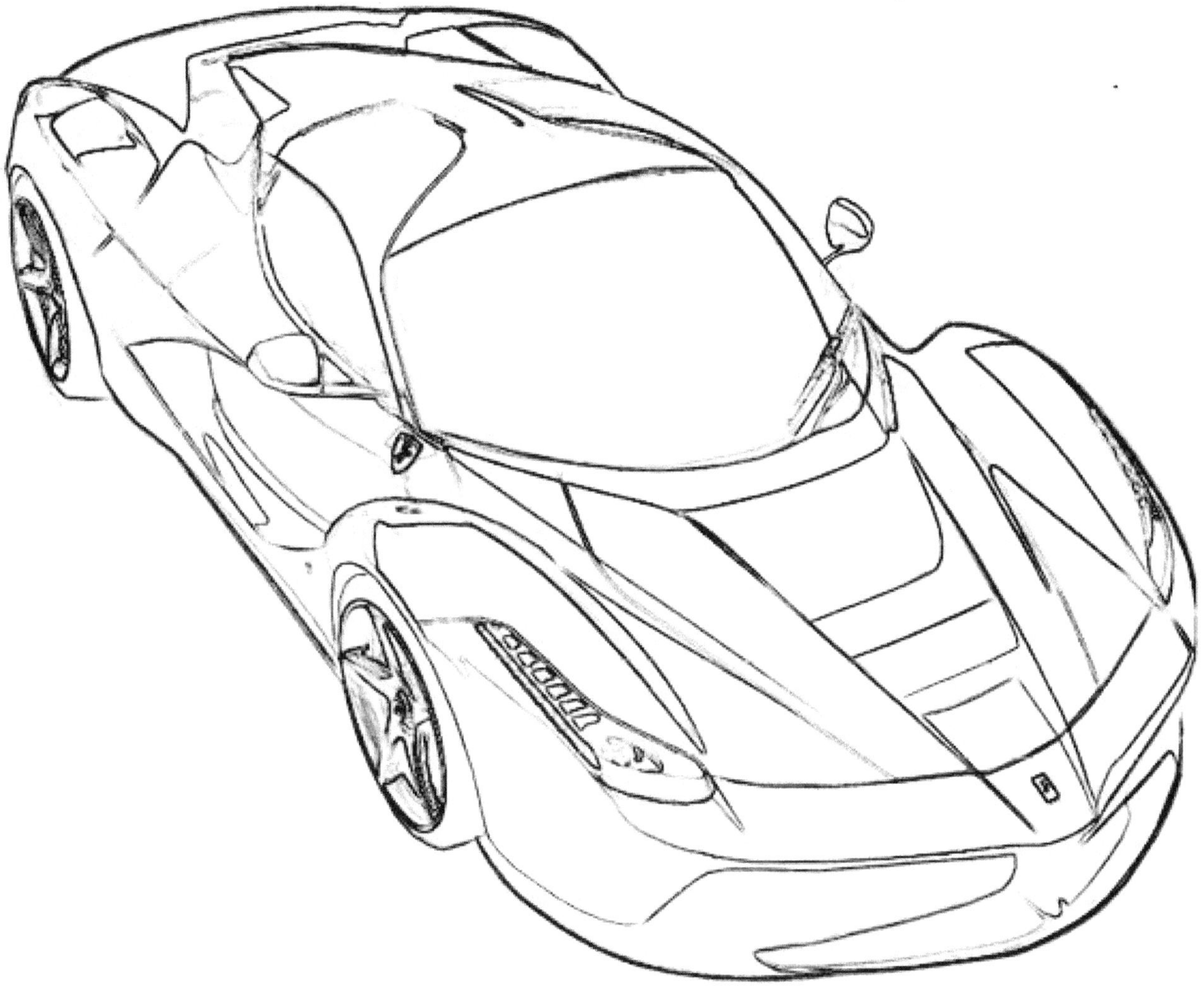

Lightning Source UK Ltd.
Milton Keynes UK
UKHW051229090821
388558UK00010B/659